THE EMPEROR HADRIAN

THE
EMPEROR HADRIAN

THORSTEN OPPER

THE BRITISH MUSEUM PRESS

© 2008 The Trustees of the British Museum

Thorsten Opper has asserted the right to be
identified as the author of this work

First published in 2008 by
The British Museum Press
A division of The British Museum Company Ltd
38 Russell Square, London WC1B 3QQ
www.britishmuseum.org

A catalogue record for this book is available
from the British Library

ISBN 978-0-7141-2266-3

Designed and typeset by Price Watkins
Printed in Italy by Graphicom Srl

Frontispiece: Marble bust of Hadrian
from his villa at Tivoli.

CONTENTS

BRITANNIA

GERMANICA
INF.

BELGICA

LUGDUNENSIS

GERMANICA
SUP.

RAETIA

NORICUM

PANNONIA
SUPERIOR

PANNONIA
INFERIOR

DACIA

AQUITANIA

ITALIA

DALMATIA

MOESIA
INFERIOR

NARBONENSIS

MOESIA
SUPERIOR

TARRACONENSIS

ALPES PENNINAE
ALPES COTTIAE
ALPES MARITIMAE

THRACIA

LUSITANIA

Rome

MACEDONIA

BAETICA

SARDINIA ET CORSICA

EPIRUS

ACHAEA

MAURETANIA
TINGITANA

MAURETANIA
CAESARENSIS

NUMIDIA

SICILIA

CRETA

ET

AFRICA

CYRENAE

N

0   500 miles
0   800 kilometres

The Roman empire at the time of Hadrian's accession in AD 117.

INTRODUCTION

Hadrian's character and legacy have fascinated people for many centuries. For nearly twenty-one years, from August AD 117 to July AD 138, he ruled one of the mightiest empires the world has ever seen. The *Imperium Romanum* enclosed parts of three continents, stretching from the Atlantic to the Euphrates, and from the Scottish lowlands to the Sahara. Hadrian took decisions that transformed the character and nature of the empire and ensured its survival for centuries to come. He was also a most remarkable individual, bristling with energy, highly gifted intellectually, with passionate, wide-ranging interests. At the same time, his character seems full of contradictions. A hardened military man and gay, he combined a surprising cultural tolerance with ruthless suppression of dissent. His rule changed history for ever, right up to today.

Publius Aelius Hadrianus was born in Rome on 24 January AD 76. No one at the time could have foretold that one day, he would be emperor. His birth in the capital was a mere coincidence, due to the residency requirements of his father, a senator from Roman Spain. Hadrian's family came from outside the traditional Roman aristocracy. Their home was Italica, a town on the River Baetis near the city of Hispalis (modern Seville) in south-west Spain. Baetica, as this

Marble bust of Hadrian
from Rome.

FOLLOWING PAGES
Roman gold coin (aureus). On the obverse is a portrait of Hadrian, on the reverse a reclining female figure who personifies the province Hispania (Spain). She holds out an olive branch, a symbol of Roman Spain's key agricultural export, olive oil.

province was called, was renowned for its natural resources, its plentiful agricultural produce and mineral wealth. Olive oil in particular, a key commodity without which the empire could not function, was among Baetica's immensely lucrative exports. All this made the region's landowning elites, to which Hadrian's family belonged, very wealthy indeed. Eventually, this economic clout brought them political influence in Rome. More and more men from the provinces, and Spain in particular, entered the senate, where they formed a close-knit, new elite.

When Hadrian was nine years old, his father died. A distant relative, his father's cousin Trajan, also a native of Italica, now became one of Hadrian's guardians. A successful general in a period of simmering conflict, Trajan's career went from strength to strength. Eventually, he was adopted by the elderly and childless emperor Nerva. When Nerva died soon after, in AD 98, Trajan became the new emperor. At a stroke, the lives of those around him, including Hadrian, were transformed.

As a teenager, Hadrian had been sent back to the family domains at Italica, where he developed a life-long passion for hunting. Taking this to excess, he was recalled to Rome, where he devoted himself to his studies and later began his political career by holding a number of prestigious junior offices. His devotion to Greek studies earned him the nickname of *Graeculus*, or little Greek. In AD 100 he married Trajan's great niece Sabina, which brought him even closer to the emperor, who had no children of his own. Trajan now embarked on a series of wars that greatly extended the empire. On the Balkans he defeated the Dacians, whose strong kingdom had long threatened Rome's borders, and occupied their territory. Hadrian, by then an experienced officer who had already served with three different legions, was by his side, first commanding a legion himself, then as governor of a key frontier province in the immediate vicinity. Trajan then annexed the kingdom of Armenia and declared war against the Parthians, Rome's eastern neighbours and traditional foes. Invading Mesopotamia (modern Iraq) and adding new provinces to the empire, he reached the Persian Gulf, bemoaning the fact that his age prevented him from continuing to India. Already, though, a large insurgency had started behind his back. Overstretched and unable to hold the ground, the Roman army fought a number of fierce battles, led by Trajan himself. Hadrian, in the meantime had been installed as governor of the province of Syria. It was here that he learnt of his adoption and Trajan's death. As the new ruler, Hadrian was faced with an empire in turmoil. He had to act rapidly and decisively. Within days, if not hours of coming to power, he withdrew the Roman army from all the territories beyond the Euphrates river. He went on to realign the empire's borders, instigate far-reaching reforms and bring stability. Forty-one years old when he came to the throne, he had already spent half of his life outside Italy. He now would spend more than half of his reign travelling the empire, tirelessly inspecting, meeting the local elites and implementing his policies in person.

Back in Rome in summer AD 118 after a long journey from the east via the Balkans, where the military situation had to be stabilized, Hadrian now embarked on a massive building programme designed to underline his legitimacy as rightful heir and ruler. He celebrated a spectacular posthumous triumph for his deified predecessor Trajan, gaining for himself the title 'son of the deified', and erected a splendid temple in his memory. In addition, he transformed the urban landscape of Rome. His passion for architecture led him to create some of the most celebrated monuments of the ancient

FOLLOWING PAGES
Hadrian's Wall.

Exterior of the Pantheon in Rome – one of the most
iconic buildings from classical antiquity. The original
Pantheon had been built by Augustus' friend and
son-in-law M. Vipsanius Agrippa in 27–25 BC, but
destroyed by fire (as had its successor building).
Hadrian rebuilt it from the ground up, but in a
studied act of modesty reinstated Agrippa's original
dedicatory inscription: *M. Agrippa L. F. Cos. Tertium
Fecit – Marcus Agrippa, Son of Lucius, three times
Consul, built this.*

world, from the Pantheon in Rome to vast palaces and entire cities. Architecture, therefore, forms a key element of Hadrian's legacy.

Hadrian recognized the strategic necessity of reaching out to the Greek population of the empire. He turned members of the Greek elite into true partners in leadership. The majority of the empire's population lived in the Greek-speaking provinces of the east. It was here that the major cities were located and the important economic centres. Situated behind the front lines of the major conflict zones, the Balkans, Caucasus, Mesopotamia and Judaea, the Greek territories formed a vital hinterland and it clearly was essential to keep the Greeks on side. However, the interest of Greeks and Romans by now largely coincided. A large Jewish Diaspora rebellion towards the end of Trajan's reign had seen both Greeks and Romans killed in their thousands in the provinces of Cyrene, Egypt and Cyprus before it was quashed by the army. Hadrian also resolved to turn Athens into the centre of a new pan-Hellenic league, intended to inject new vitality into the old, proud cities of the Greek world. In the process, he transformed Athens from the sleepy heritage site and university town it had become into the religious and cultural centre of a revitalized Greek east.

Hadrian went on two extended tours of the empire. The first, lasting from AD 121 to 125, took him to the northern and western provinces, before looming conflict in the east called him there. A military show of strength combined with extensive diplomacy, the hallmarks of Hadrian's foreign policy, averted a new war with the Parthians. This allowed him to continue his journey with a tour of the eastern provinces. From AD 128 to 132 he went to Africa and again to the east, including an extended stay in Greece. In total, there are only five provinces of his vast empire that at present he cannot be proven to have visited.

In AD 122 Hadrian visited Britain. He had come from Germany, where he had inspected border defences. The situation in the province of Britain appears to have been highly volatile. Various sources hint at ongoing problems with rebellious tribes and unremitting military activity, but any specific detail is lacking. Hadrian now decided to mark the spine of the existing deep frontier zone in the north of England with a continuous rampart, most of it built from stone. The ensuing security barrier, now known as Hadrian's Wall, is one of the most famous monuments associated with his name. Yet the Wall was not simply a defensive bulwark, constructed to 'separate Romans and barbarians' as a later source has it, but an aggressive tool of Roman dominance that allowed the military and economic control of a wide area and had a deep psychological impact on the local tribes.

In AD 136, suffering from a serious illness and without natural heirs, Hadrian decided to adopt a successor. His first choice fell on one of the consuls of that year, Lucius Ceionius Commodus. However, the new heir was an ill man himself and died less than a year later. Hadrian therefore implemented an even more far-reaching arrangement. He adopted the wealthy aristocrat Antoninus Pius, who in turn had to adopt the young Lucius Verus and Marcus Aurelius. Thus, the succession at a stroke was secured over two generations.

Hadrian died on 10 July AD 138. His reign left a deep mark on the Roman empire. He consolidated it at a time of crisis and provided it with a vital breathing space, while his various economic, military and legal reforms strengthened it from within.

RIGHT
Interior view of the Pantheon, with its magnificent concrete dome.
FOLLOWING PAGES
Hadrian's mausoleum in Rome.

THE NEW EMPEROR

Hadrian was proclaimed emperor on 11 August AD 117, having been adopted by Trajan on his deathbed. While Trajan had shown Hadrian clear signs of favour over the years, he had never made him the heir apparent by bestowing on him the title of Caesar. On the contrary, he had repeatedly suggested that there might be a number of worthy successors should his life come to an end. This ambiguity, together with misgivings over Hadrian's immediate redrawing of the empire's eastern borders, led to rumours questioning the legitimacy of Trajan's official adoption of Hadrian – it was said by some that it had been manipulated by Trajan's wife Plotina, who was well inclined towards Hadrian. A number of senators appear to have plotted against him and were executed. While Hadrian denied all responsibility for this act, it overshadowed his relations with the senate for much of his reign.

Marble portrait bust of Trajan (r. AD 98–117). Clean-shaven and with a simple hairstyle, he appears as an energetic, no-nonsense military leader.

Aureus of Hadrian. On the obverse a portrait of Hadrian in a very unusual portrait type; on the reverse, portraits of his deified adoptive parents Trajan and Plotina. The coin issue is dated to after AD 128, when Hadrian assumed the title of *Pater Patriae*, 'Father of the Fatherland'. This is hard to reconcile with the very youthful-looking portrait on the obverse.

A sardonyx cameo with a finely carved double portrait of Trajan and Plotina. Such precious objects, often made by expert craftsmen from the Greek east, were circulated among the elite.

AN EMPIRE IN TURMOIL

Trajan was celebrated as a great conqueror, a living embodiment of the Roman concept of *imperium sine fine*, an empire without boundaries. This coin shows him standing triumphant over the subdued personification of Armenia, who is flanked by two river gods – the Euphrates and Tigris. It graphically proclaims Trajan's recent victories in the east and was one of many issued to advertise his conquests and diplomatic triumphs. In the face of such propaganda, it was difficult for the Roman public to come to terms with the sudden military reversals and Hadrian's immediate abandonment of many of the newly conquered territories. Reality for Hadrian, however, was a disastrous military situation in a substantial part of the empire: 'The nations conquered by Trajan were in revolt; the Moors were on a rampage; the Britons could not be kept under Roman sovereignty; Egypt was ravaged by uprisings; finally, Libya and Palestine displayed their spirit of rebellion.' (*Historia Augusta*, Hadrian 5.2)

PORTRAITURE AND PUBLIC IMAGE

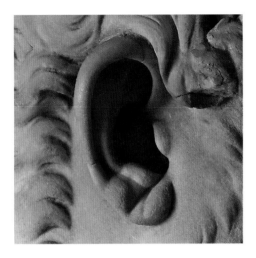

All portraits of Hadrian show a surprising anatomical detail that occurs in real life: a very marked, diagonal earlobe crease. This can help specialists to tell genuine, authentic portraits of Hadrian from those of contemporaries emulating his appearance as well as from modern replicas or forgeries. In medical terms, there is a strong statistical link between the occurrence of diagonal creases in both earlobes and coronary artery disease. It therefore seems possible that Hadrian suffered from this illness. The existence of such a life-like detail lends Hadrian's portrait a dramatic immediacy.

Bust of Hadrian in military attire from his villa at Tivoli.

HADRIAN IN THE GREEK MANTLE

This statue is made up of fragments discovered in 1861 in the Temple of Apollo in the city of Cyrene in northern Africa. Here, Hadrian wears the *himation*, the Greek mantle. The statue is unique and has become very famous as it seems perfectly to embody the concept of Hadrian as a philhellene, an ardent admirer of Greek culture. However, doubts about the lack of parallels for such a representation of the emperor have led to a recent re-examination of the statue, and it is now clear that the head and body never belonged together – they are the result of an incorrect Victorian restoration. As this statue can physically be exploded, so can much of the myth of Hadrian as a peaceful philhellene.

In Roman iconography, the emperor could only be represented in a very limited number of officially sanctioned ways: in the toga, the civilian state costume; in military attire, as commander-in-chief; or nude, likened to a god.

HEAD OF THE CYRENE STATUE

The head of the Cyrene statue has recently been separated from the body. Originally it must have been inserted into a different statue or bust, where carved drapery would have covered much of the neck.

Hadrian was the first Roman emperor to wear a full beard. This, too, has been interpreted as a sign of his infatuation with Greek culture, in that he wanted to appear like a Greek from the Classical past. However, more recently it has been pointed out that many soldiers wore beards, at least during campaigns, and that he may therefore appear as a young general interested in promoting his military credentials. A much more prosaic explanation is given by the *Historia Augusta*, an ancient source on Hadrian's life: it claims that he wore a beard to hide facial blemishes.

STATUE OF HADRIAN FROM HIERAPYTNA ON CRETE

Hadrian, crowned by a wreath and wearing the battle dress of a Roman general, tramples underfoot a defeated barbarian. This statuary type was particularly common in the Greek east. At first sight, it could be understood as representing the menacing face of Roman dominance. However, after the recent rebellions against Roman rule – for example by the diaspora Jews, from which Greeks and Romans had suffered in equal measure – it offered reassurance. Hadrian appears here as the protector from a common foe. The decoration of the body armour reinforces this message (see overleaf): the goddess Athena (the Roman Minerva), crowned by two winged victory goddesses, stands on a Roman she-wolf, symbolizing the new union between Greece and Rome.

FOLLOWING PAGES
Details of statue.

THE MILITARY LEADER

This coin shows Hadrian personally leading Roman soldiers. He is followed by standard bearers and a legionary. Undoubtedly due to the influence of his guardian Trajan, Hadrian had followed a thorough military career before he became emperor. He served as a military tribune with three different legions, instead of only one or two as was customary, and later commanded a legion himself during one of Trajan's wars. Several ancient writers stress his familiarity with military life and easy-going manner with common soldiers.

Much of Hadrian's time travelling the empire was taken up with the inspection of army units in key frontier provinces. This was regularly commemorated on coins. On the coin illustrated overleaf he is seen addressing the troops of the army in Britain ('*exercitus Britannicus*'), where three Roman legions and substantial numbers of non-citizens auxiliary forces were stationed.

One ancient writer states that 'both by his example and by his precepts he so trained and disciplined the whole military force throughout the entire empire that even today the methods then introduced by him are the soldiers' law of campaigning. This best explains why he lived for the most part at peace with foreign nations ....'

FOLLOWING PAGES
**Coin showing Hadrian
addressing the army of Britain.**

BRONZE HEAD FROM THE RIVER THAMES

This remarkable bronze portrait head was recovered from the River Thames near the old London Bridge in 1834. It is the only large-scale portrait of Hadrian that survives from Britain. The head originally probably belonged to a full-length statue that may have stood on the Roman bridge over the Thames or in an important public square, such as the forum of Londinium, not far away. The head appears to have been made in a local workshop and differs from Roman metropolitan models in a number of details. It has been argued that the craftsman who produced it had to work from a two-dimensional source, such as a coin. However, Hadrian's characteristic earlobe creases are clearly marked.

CEREMONIAL CAVALRY HELMET

Roman cavalry units regularly staged elaborate mock battles, so-called *hippica gymnasia* (mounted exercises). Clad in splendid parade armour and using blunted weapons, the elite horsemen of the unit competed against each other in two groups.

This helmet was discovered together with other items, mainly military awards and horse trappings, under the floorboards of a building in the Roman fort at Ribchester, Lancashire. It is decorated with scenes of battle between mounted warriors and others on foot.

Numerous cavalry units were stationed along Hadrian's Wall. Highly mobile, they allowed the efficient control of the deep frontier zone on either side. The unit stationed at Ribchester in Hadrian's time came from Asturia in Roman Spain.

A SOUVENIR FROM HADRIAN'S WALL?

The so-called 'Staffordshire Moorlands Pan' belongs to a group of closely related bronze *trullae* (pans) that provides information on Hadrian's Wall and the lives of people who were stationed there. These *trullae* were made near the Wall by craftsmen working perhaps largely for a military clientele in the middle of the second century

AD and later. Skilfully enamelled in the colours blue, red and green, they attest the high level of craftsmanship in the area. They are remarkably alike in shape and size, and all are inscribed with the names of forts along the western end of the Wall. They may have served as special souvenirs from the frontier, perhaps even as retirement gifts for military personnel.

AUGUSTUS

Hadrian chose Rome's first emperor, Augustus (r. 27 BC – AD 14), as an important role model. He used a portrait of Augustus on his signet ring and kept a small bronze bust of the emperor among the images of the household gods in his bedroom.

One of the reasons may have been that after severe military setbacks, Augustus had to renounce any further expansion of the empire and instead concentrate on diplomacy, implementing measures similar to the ones pursued by Hadrian after his own accession. This added legitimacy to Hadrian's policies.

THE JEWISH REBELLION

Hadrian was a great military leader and strategist, but this episode shows a very different facet of his character: Romans as perpetrators of extreme violence and destruction, not a civilizing power.

Hadrian's decision to re-found Jerusalem with Roman settlers as the new colony of Aelia Capitolina sparked off a fierce Jewish revolt that lasted from AD 132 to 136. His plans for Aelia Capitolina for ever denied the Jewish people the opportunity to rebuild their Temple, the centre of Jewish religion and identity, which had been destroyed by the Romans a generation earlier.

Taking the occupying power by surprise, the Jews established for a time a liberated territory under their leader Simon Bar Kokhba. The Roman governor of Britain was sent to Judaea to take command of the army with reinforcements rushed in from throughout the empire. In the end, the rebellion was brutally quashed. 'Fifty of their most important outposts and 985 of their better known villages were razed to the ground. 585000 were killed in the various engagements or battles. As for the numbers who perished from starvation, disease or fire, that was impossible to establish,' the Roman historian Cassius Dio states about the defeated Jews. The consequences were far-reaching. Jews were permanently expelled from Judaea and the name of the province was changed to Syria-Palaestina.

Bronze head of Hadrian from the legionary camp at Tel Shalem.

A magnificent bronze statue of Hadrian discovered in a Roman fort at Tel Shalem in the Jordan valley may belong in this context. However, the decoration of the body armour, with nude warriors locked in fierce combat, is highly unusual and may infer that the head and torso did not originally belong together.

The rebels and members of the Jewish civilian population fled to underground hideouts and caves in the Judaean desert. There, the arid climate has preserved their belongings remarkably well (see overleaf). The so-called Cave of Letters contained handwritten documents by Bar Kokhba, and many objects that the Jewish refugees took with them. Among these were the keys with which they had locked their houses, clearly hoping to return – yet they all perished.

Palm-fibre basket, wooden plate, knife and keys with wooden handles, and bronze jugs from the Cave of Letters. Due to the arid desert climate, organic material from the cave is extraordinarily well preserved.

This bronze *patera*, an implement for liquid offerings during religious rituals, is one of several objects from the Cave of Letters decorated with scenes from Graeco-Roman mythology. Here, the nymph Thetis, mother of the Greek hero Achilles, is shown riding on the back of a sea creature. The occurrence of such objects among a group of Jewish refugees is surprising. Perhaps they were taken as booty from the Romans, or the people hiding in the cave included non-Jewish rebels.

A PASSION FOR ARCHITECTURE

Hadrian had a keen personal interest in architecture. He was part of a social class whose members routinely commissioned buildings either as private patrons or through the political offices they held, and followed developments with close interest. A well-known, but quite possibly invented anecdote has him interrupting a conversation between Trajan and his famous master of works, the military engineer and architect Apollodorus of Damascus. Apollodorus told him to 'go draw your pumpkins', dismissively referring to a sketch Hadrian had made. Rumours had it that he never forgave Apollodorus and had him exiled or even executed after a further slight, but there is little to substantiate this story. As it happened, Hadrian lived through an exciting period of breakneck development in the Roman building industry that saw great advances particularly in concrete technology. This allowed the construction of buildings never seen before in human history. Most commentators now believe that the sketch must have been the design of a ribbed dome in the latest concrete technology that Hadrian had made.

A richly decorated marble frieze from the so-called Basilica of Neptune in Rome. The Basilica, located immediately behind the Pantheon, was one of many monuments Hadrian built or restored in the area. The carved frieze, with dolphins and sea shells, closely resembles similar architectural elements from Hadrian's villa at Tivoli.

This marble capital comes from the interior of the Pantheon. Originally it crowned a pilaster made of porphyry, a rare and very expensive purple stone, in the upper zone of the Pantheon rotunda's inner wall. This part of the monument was altered in the mid-eighteenth century and the capitals were removed.

HADRIAN'S VILLA

Near the town of Tibur (modern Tivoli), some 28 km east of Rome, Hadrian built a magnificent country residence, the largest villa known from the Roman world. A vast architectural playground, with baths and theatres fit for a small town, this was where he carried out government business and frequently entertained large numbers of guests. In common with aristocratic Roman tradition, he named parts of the villa after famous sites and monuments in the empire. From the

Renaissance on, the villa became a focal point for artists and architects who aimed to rediscover the splendour of ancient Rome. New excavations carried out within the last few years have led to a number of spectacular discoveries, including a memorial to Hadrian's lover Antinous, situated along one of the main access routes. Recent systematic studies also enable us to understand the working mechanisms of the site.

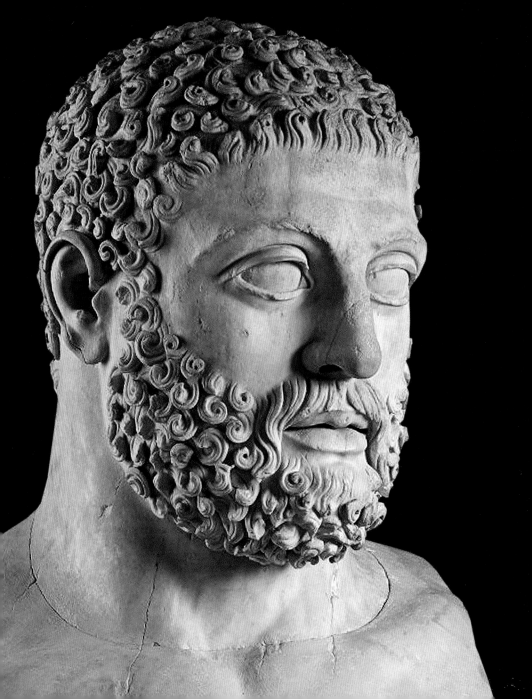

DECORATIVE DETAILS

Hadrian's villa was richly decorated with works of art, defining indoor and outdoor spaces and imbuing them with allegorical meaning. Copies of famous masterpieces from the Greek past were prominent and underlined Rome's mission as powerful guardian of this classical heritage.

Colossal bust of Hercules from Hadrian's villa. The style is reminiscent of Greek works of the early fifth century BC.

Pillar decorated with a long, leafy branch
and scenes of birds and other animals.

OVERLEAF
An ornate black-and-white mosaic from
one of the villa's quarters assigned to
guests or high-ranking staff.

Relief from the villa showing a boy restraining a horse, accompanied by a dog. The composition dates to Hadrian's time, but draws on models from fifth-century Greece, such as the Parthenon frieze.

ANTINOUS

The nature of Hadrian's sexuality has been the subject of much speculation and continues to occupy his biographers to this day. To ordinary Romans it mattered little. If anything set Hadrian apart, it was that his name became forever associated with one particular individual: Antinous, a young Greek in his entourage. When Antinous drowned in the Nile in October AD 130, Hadrian mourned him with unusual intensity and encouraged his cult in the eastern empire. At the centre of this cult was the belief that, like the ancient Egyptian god Osiris, Antinous had been reborn from the waters of the Nile. Its centre was the new city of Antinoopolis, founded on the right bank of the Nile close to the spot where Antinous had drowned and named in his memory. Remarkable images of Hadrian's late favourite were set up by the emperor himself and by many members of the elite, especially in the Greek east, where this was a new way of showing loyalty to Hadrian while at the same time celebrating the participants' Greek identity.

Head from a statue that showed Antinous as Dionysus, the closest Greek equivalent to the Egyptian god Osiris.

IMAGES OF ANTINOUS

Depending on their intended setting, many different types of Antinous statues were created in the years following his death. Antinous was likened to an array of different gods, from Osiris himself and the closest Greek equivalent Dionysus to minor deities like Sylvanus and Autumnus. Busts and small statues were made for domestic settings, colossal statues for religious shrines. There were also reliefs and more intimate objects, such as gems, bearing his portrait, and many Greek cities issued coins with his image.

About one hundred marble images of Antinous are currently known to archaeologists. They turn his portrait type into one of the most powerful legacies from classical antiquity, in numbers only surpassed by the images of the Emperor Augustus and Hadrian himself.

This statue shows Antinous as Osiris, reborn from the waters of the Nile. New research indicates that it comes from the memorial built for Antinous at Hadrian's villa near Tivoli.

GRIEF PORTRAYED

Hadrian clearly felt a strong need to surround himself with Antinous' images and thereby perpetuate his presence. His suffering and intense sense of bereavement are nowhere more obvious than at the great villa at Tivoli. At least ten marble images of Antinous were found there. Archaeologists have also recently discovered the remains of a possible monumental tomb or cenotaph for Antinous himself – the 'Antinoeion' – along one of the main access routes to the villa.

Detail of the Antinous-Osiris statue. There is a titillating contrast between Antinous' soft, sensuous face and his muscular body.

SABINA

In the accounts of Hadrian's life, his wife and empress, Vibia Sabina, remains mostly in the shadows. She was born in about AD 86, the daughter of Trajan's beloved niece Matidia. The marriage between Sabina and Hadrian was arranged in about AD 100, not long after Trajan acceded to the throne. Sabina was probably about fourteen, the typical age for Roman brides, and Hadrian twenty-four. It would turn out to be a loveless union, but was obviously politically advantageous for Hadrian. Although their personal relationship was strained, Hadrian treated Sabina with deference in public. She was honoured with numerous statues and her image was put on coins. After her death, Hadrian asked the senate to deify Sabina officially.

Detail from over-lifesized portrait statue of Sabina, probably posthumous (see overleaf).

FAR LEFT **The aureus was struck to commemorate Sabina's deification. It shows her portrait on the obverse and an eagle bearing her to the heavens on the reverse.**

LEFT AND BELOW **This statue of Sabina still shows traces of pigment – originally, all marble sculptures were painted.**

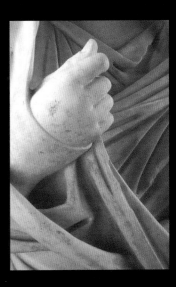

DEATH AND SUCCESSION

Hadrian and Sabina did not have any children, so, as he himself had been adopted by Trajan, Hadrian decided to adopt a worthy successor. His choice eventually fell on the wealthy aristocrat Antoninus Pius, who had been a member of the imperial council and Hadrian's close confidant for many years. Antoninus, in turn, was obliged to adopt the seven-year-old Lucius Verus and the sixteen-year-old Marcus Aurelius. Thus the succession was secured over two generations.

A papyrus fragment discovered in the Fayum region of Egypt preserves a few lines of text that have been plausibly interpreted as the only extant excerpt of Hadrian's lost autobiography. Written shortly before Hadrian's death, this autobiography appears to have taken the form of a series of letters to Antoninus.

Portrait bust of Antoninus Pius, who was adopted by Hadrian in February AD **138.**

MARCUS AURELIUS

Hadrian was much taken by the young Marcus Annius Verus (the future Marcus Aurelius), whom he called *Verissimus*, the Truest or Sincerest. Marcus came from a family from Roman Spain closely linked to Hadrian's own. It seems likely that this portrait bust shows Marcus at the time of his adoption, when he was not yet seventeen.

LUCIUS VERUS

Lucius was the son of Hadrian's first adopted heir, Lucius Ceionius Commodus, who died in January AD 138. The portrait type used for this bust was created as a pendant to that of Marcus, probably to celebrate their adoption. It beautifully captures his youth and refined upbringing.

HADRIAN'S MAUSOLEUM

Hadrian died on 10 July AD 138 at Baiae on the Gulf of Naples and was initially buried at nearby Puteoli. Later his body was transferred to his mausoleum (now the Castel Sant'Angelo, see pages 20–21), situated on the right bank of the River Tiber in Rome. Probably begun early in his reign, the mausoleum set out Hadrian's claim to establish an enduring new dynasty. It also reassured the Roman public about his intentions towards the capital while he devoted much of his time to travelling the empire. Linked to the city by a new bridge, the Pons Aelius, the mausoleum was splendidly decorated and dominated its surroundings. These remarkable peacocks (illustrated opposite and on the following pages) are made of gilded bronze. They probably stood on a fence that surrounded the mausoleum and give an idea of the lavish decoration of the monument. The Romans linked peacocks with the goddess Juno, wife of their supreme god Jupiter. Peacocks were also associated with the empress and later were used as a symbol for her deification, just as the eagle stood for the deification of the emperor (see pages 92–3). The survival of these sculptures is due to their use by the Popes. In the medieval period, they decorated a fountain outside the old Basilica of St Peter.

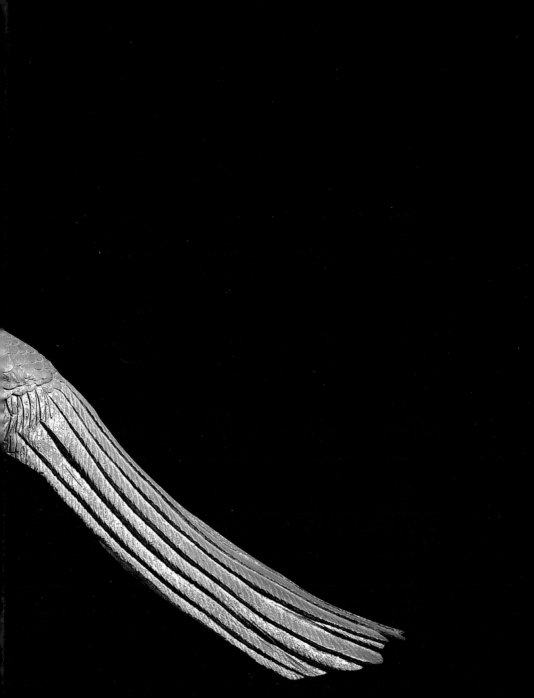

Gold coin minted to commemorate Hadrian's deification, which involved a spectacular public ceremony in the centre of Rome.

FURTHER READING

A.R. Birley, *Hadrian: The Restless Emperor* (London/New York 1997).

M.T. Boatwright, *Hadrian and the City of Rome* (Princeton 1987).

M.T. Boatwright, *Hadrian and the Cities of the Roman Empire* (Princeton 2000).

D. Danziger and N. Purcell, *Hadrian's Empire: When Rome Ruled the World* (London 2005).

W. MacDonald and J. Pinto, *Hadrian's Villa and its Legacy* (New Haven 1995).

T. Opper, *Hadrian: Empire and Conflict* (London 2008).

E. Speller, *Following Hadrian: A second-century-journey through the Roman Empire* (London 2002).

M. Yourcenar, *Memoirs of Hadrian* (trans. London and New York 1954).

ILLUSTRATION ACKNOWLEDGEMENTS

Frontispiece: The Trustees of the British Museum; GR 1805,0703.95 (photo John Williams and Saul Peckham)
Map p. 6: The Trustees of the British Museum (artwork Paul Goodhead).
p. 8: The Trustees of the British Museum; GR 1805,0703.94 (photo John Williams and Saul Peckham)
pp. 10–11: The Trustees of the British Museum; BMC Hadrian 843
pp. 14–15: Roger Clegg
p. 16: The Trustees of the British Museum (photo John Williams and Saul Peckham)
p. 19: The Trustees of the British Museum (photo John Williams and Saul Peckham)
pp. 20–21: The Trustees of the British Museum (photo John Williams and Saul Peckham)
p. 23: The Trustees of the British Museum; GR 1805,0703.93 (photo John Williams and Saul Peckham)
p. 24: The Trustees of the British Museum; CM 1850,0601.4
p. 25: The Trustees of the British Museum; GR 1824,0301.97
p. 27: The Trustees of the British Museum; BM Trajan 613
pp. 28–9: The Trustees of the British Museum; GR 1805,0703.95 (photo John Williams and Saul Peckham)
pp. 31–2: The Trustees of the British Museum; GR 1861,1127.23 (photo John Williams and Saul Peckham)
pp. 34–7: Museo della Civiltà Romana; inv. no. 395 (photo John Williams and Saul Peckham)
p. 38 The Trustees of the British Museum; BMC Hadrian 1484
pp. 40–41: G. Cope Collection (photo The Trustees of the British Museum)
p. 42: The Trustees of the British Museum; PE 1848,1103.1 (photo John Williams and Saul Peckham)
p. 45: The Trustees of the British Museum; PE 1814,0705.1
pp. 46–7: The Trustees of the British Museum; PE 2005,1204.1
p. 48: The Trustees of the British Museum; GR 1812,0615.1 (photo John Williams and Saul Peckham)
pp. 51–3: Collection The Israel Antiquities Authority, Jerusalem; inv. nos IDAM 75-763 (head) and 75-764 (cuirass). Photograph © The Israel Museum, Jerusalem (John Williams and Saul Peckham)
pp. 54–5: Collection The Israel Antiquities